Anchored Soul

by

W.B. Godbey

First Fruits Press
Wilmore,
Kentucky
c2017

Anchored Soul. By W.B. Godbey.
First Fruits Press, © 2017

ISBN: 9781621717287 (paperback), 9781621717294 (digital), 9781621717300
(kindle)

Digital version at http://place.asburyseminary.edu/godbey/6/

For all other uses, contact:

First Fruits Press
B.L. Fisher Library
Asbury Theological Seminary
204 N. Lexington Ave.
Wilmore, KY 40390
http://place.asburyseminary.edu/firstfruits

Godbey, W. B. (William Baxter), 1833-1920.
   Anchored soul / by W.B. Godbey. – Wilmore, KY : First Fruits Press,
©2017.
      35 pages ; cm.
      Reprint. Previously published: Greensboro, N.C. : Apostolic Messenger
Office, [190-?].
      ISBN: 9781621717287 (pbk.)
      1. Holiness. I. Title.
BT767.G622 2017   234.8

Cover design by Jon Ramsey

asburyseminary.edu
800.2ASBURY
204 North Lexington Avenue
Wilmore, Kentucky 40390

First Fruits
THE ACADEMIC OPEN PRESS OF ASBURY SEMINARY

First Fruits Press
The Academic Open Press of Asbury Theological Seminary
204 N. Lexington Ave., Wilmore, KY 40390
859-858-2236
first.fruits@asburyseminary.edu
asbury.to/firstfruits

Anchored Soul

By

W. B. Godbey

AUTHOR OF
"New Testament Commentaries" "New Testament
Translation," and a great number of
other books and booklets.

PUBLISHED BY

APOSTOLIC MESSENGER OFFICE

900 SILVER RUN AVE.

GREENSBORO, N. C.

Anchored Soul

Hebrews ~~fourth~~ chapter gives us this beautiful simile of a ship afloat on the ocean, amid howling storms, desolating hurricanes, spinning cyclones and wasting tornadoes, dashing her hither and thither, tossing her topsy turvy high up toward the stars; meanwhile falling back she sinks deep down into the briny abyss and seems surely lost as she is entirely out of sight; but she comes again only to receive another embrace in the jolly cyclone playing with her like a boy spins his top, simultaneously with the tremendous sweep of the hurricane as he moves on his precipitated pinions over the dark lined deep. Spectators on the shore says, "Good-bye ship, there is no chance for you, but to find a sepulchre in the bottom of the briny deep, where the sea-weeds will envelop you in their cordial embraces to hug you only the tighter, as the centuries come and go, and the monsters inhabiting the oceanic forests will find in thee a resting-place, where they will recuperate their strength and reinvigorate for grander campaigns, chasing the finny tribes of the deep; the magnitudinous whale, the voracious shark and the stalwart walrus, finding about thee a place to rest their weary muscles ever and anon. The ship here symbolizes the human soul; the ocean, this wicked world, by diabolical armies invaded from the rising of the sun to the going down of the same, from pole to pole, by land and sea. The mortality is the whale, the ravines between us and the haven of eternal rest and ineffable bliss. We cast the anchor, which is our hope of heaven through this veil into the glory realm and it takes fast hold of Jesus the great Rock of Ages. The anchor cast down to the bottom of the sea, is so big and heavy that it takes hold of the rocks and holds the ship, despite all the storms which toss it hither and thither, capsizing and inundating it. But it is so solidly built as to be storm proof. If it were not for the anchor, these cyclones and blizzards would carry it away, dash it against the rocks, smashing it into smitherines so it would never be seen again, but flounder to the bottom of the sea and receive interment beneath the rolling sandbars.

When we reached Joppa, Palestine in 1911, a great storm was on the sea so that we couldn't land, but had to sail around in a circle; the land of Canaan, for which we so long sighed, in plain view; the great Mediterranean plain stretching out twenty miles to the majestic mountains of Judah and Benjamin, so celebrated in the Bible by the miracles wrought by Samson, David and the armies of Israel. Thirty-six hours we moved round on that circle; multitudes on board awfully seasick and among them the most of my party, consisting of eight Holiness preachers. What a dreary time! as we could not land. Meanwhile I asked why they did not cast anchor. The captain answered that the storm was so high he was afraid he would lose his anchor. As Jonah had sailed from that same port, Joppa, and over that same sea, swept by an awful storm, threatening to bury the ship in the bottom of the deep; my people were talking about it and wondering if the whale was there ready to swallow them in case we should go down, as he did Jonah. In our return tour it was our privilege to run on the track of Jonah who was sailing to Tarshish. (As there are no whales in the Mediterranean, infidels have brought that up against the Bible. While that is true, there are plenty of sharks in it which are amply competent to swallow a man. We saw a great school of sharks near Tarsus as we ran by. Besides, the Bible does say it was a whale. The word **cetus** there used, simply means a sea monster.)

Bunyan's Pilgrim, as he journeyed from the city

of destruction to the celestial city, was accompanied
by Faithful, who traveled with him till they reached
Vanity Fair, where they raised an awful hubbub,
prosecuted and condemned them, burning Faithful
at the stake, out of whose ashes Hopeful sprang up,
became his traveling companion and accompanied
him all the way through to the Celestial City. Here
you see Hopeful spring from the ashes of Faithful,
showing that when your faith is made perfect so that
you are ready for martyrdom, then Hope springs up
spontaneously. In our text hope is the anchor of
the soul, sure and steadfast, caught fast in the Rock
which is within the veil, so when our faith is made
perfect by the baptism of the Holy Ghost, which
burns up Satan's ladder consisting of six steps, all
beginning with "d," because "devil" begins with "d":
doubt, discouragement, despondency, despair, death,
damnation. When Jesus baptizes you, the fires of
the Holy Ghost burn up the devil's ladder, so your
faith is thereby made perfect, i. e., free from doubt
and all this dark catalogue; thus preparing you for
martyrdom. Then hope mounts upon the wing,
soars and towers and flickers at nothing; regardless
of environments, doubts, fears, despondency, the
blues and every phase of discouragement; your hope
has the victory and shouts aloud amid roaring
storms, raging tempests, wasting hurricanes, wither-
ing siroccoes and pestiferous simoons. Therefore
when your faith is made perfect by the baptism of the
Holy Ghost, hope rises on radiant wing and sings
her song of victory and is here beautifully symbolized by the anchor cast from the ship down into the
dark deep sea; whose cerulean abyss no human eye
can penetrate. Therefore you see your anchor no
more. Hope is not for this life but that which is to
come. It flies away to heaven, its glorious destina-
tion our heroic pioneer, to explore the way for our
triumphant ingress, when this stormy voyage shall

wind to a close and we round the cape into the
harbor and responsively to the shout of the Captain,
"New Jerusalem," all disembark. Already Hope
has been there ever since the Lord baptized us with
the Holy Ghost and prepared us for the martyrdom,
to shine and shout and press the battle for Him in
this world, or joyfully seal our faith with our blood.
Hence you see from this metaphor the beautiful attitude of the sanctified soul in this life, symbolized
by the ship, while the ocean typifies this wicked
world, racked with storms and swept by tempests;
meanwhile we are perfectly safe as we have cast our
anchor beyond the vale of mortality, whither we enter when we pass through the Valley of the Shad-
dow of Death (Ps. 23 ch.) ; the bright angel of Hope
already awaiting us and ready to introduce us to
the jubilant heavenly host; having been there triumphant in the arms of Jesus ever since our sanctification; meanwhile we were fighting the battles
on the stormy seas and bloody continents of this
lost world.

Chapter I.

THIS STORMY VOYAGE

When in A. D. 68 Rome took fire and burned
like an ocean of flame six days and seven nights;
Nero, the demonized Emperor, sat on a lofty
tower, played his fiddle and sang the "Destruction of Troy"; thus treating that awful calamity so
levitously, as to impress all the people that he had
ordered the conflagration. To rid himself of the
direful accusation, he laid it on the Christians, con-
demning all to die for the double treason against the
government and heresy against all the Roman gods.
Having sent away to Nicapolis, in northern Greece,
arrested Paul, brought him thither and incarcerated
him in that awful mamertine prison excavated in a
great stratum at the base of the Capoline Mountains;
nicely cleaned off, when they drilled through and go
down and excavate a great apartment beneath the
rock, with no entrance except the circular aperture
at the top; thus forming a great prison, the most
indefrigable in all the world and used by them for
the incarceration of the worst criminals against the
government. In it they incarcerate Paul and Peter.
[Paul first and Peter afterward.] When they got
ready to lead Paul out he stands before Nero in
the old Judgment Hall on the Palatine Mountain,
where he is condemned to die. As he is a Roman
citizen they cannot crucify him. They lead him
away through the gate of the city, two and one-half
miles and give him a private execution, decapitating
him with a sword. They say when they cut off his
head it bounded twenty feet and struck the ground;
a fountain of living water leaping out and flowing
to this day. Then it bounded again and struck

twenty feet distant; another fountain leaping out
and still flowing, also bounding the third time and
striking the earth, when another leaps up and is
still flowing. I have drunk out of all of them and
found the water splendid.

When they had beheaded Paul, the saints so ear-
nestly importuned Peter to make his escape so he
could live to take care of the Church. Having acqui-
esced, he is walking rapidly in the dead of the night
along the Appian Way, over which Paul entered the
city, when they sent him thither from Jerusalem
for trial. Suddenly Jesus comes meeting him, walking rapidly into the city; when Peter says to Him:
Domine quo avis, "Lord whither goest Thou?" He
responds, "Peter, I am coming to Rome to be crucified again," that moment vanishing from his sight.
Peter turns back and tells the saints that Jesus had
met him and notified him that he is to be crucified
in Rome.

(a) Consequently they arrest, prosecute and con-
demn him to be crucified **Campus Martius,** by his own
request with his head down, alleging that he was
unworthy to be crucified in the posture of his Lord
as he had once denied Him. If you ever go to Rome
you will visit the Cathedral of St. Peter on that
very spot, 835 feet long, 330 feet wide, 448 feet high,
with auditory capacity for fifty thousand. You will
find his sepulchre in the centre, lights burning all
around it which never go out. I have often been
there and seen his gold coffin. His bronze statue
stands near without, whose feet the pilgrims kiss
till they have almost worn all his toes off.

(b) While Rome was burning the awful Jewish
Tribulation was doing its bloody work; exterminating all the Jews out of Palestine and selling them
into slavery to all nations, gathered thither to supply
themselves. At Jerusalem alone a million perish by
the sword, pestilence and famine and ninety thou-

sand are sold into slavery; leaving on their hands an immense host, who are led captive to Rome and turned over as the Crown Slaves of the Emperor. He puts them to building public works, among them they build the Colosseum the largest theatre ever built in the world: 1800 feet in circumference, 160 feet high, solid wall up to the eve and seating capacity for 100,000 spectators; eliptical in shape, having the properties of a whispering gallery with two foci and pronounced one of the Seven Wonders of the World.

(e)   After Nero had passed that edict of extermination against all the Christians they adopted the plan of feeding them to their wild beasts: quite a convenience as they had quite a number of them in their lairs in the Palatine Mountain, hard by the Colosseum.   As they brought them through the north gate, they called it the gate of life and carried out their bones after they had been devoured by the wild beasts, through the south gate, which they called the gate of death.   Oh, the wagon loads of money poured into the imperial treasury by the 100,000 spectators, daily crowding the Colosseum to see the wild beasts eat up the Christians.

I have often looked into the old tunnel through which they brought out the lions, leopards, tigers, hyenas and wolves; coming roaring and screaming; so hungry for their dinners, on purpose to make them awfully voracious, so they would devour them with the utmost greediness.   When they brought old Ignatius. the successor of Polycarp, the successor of the Apostle John, all the way from Ephesus to cast him to the wild beasts; the Emperor Trajan because he was 100 years old, waiting on him in person; begging him to recant, observing that it broke his heart to see a man so old cast to the wild beasts; when he responded: "You rule the whole world.   I would not swap places with you if I could.   I would rather die

for Jesus than to rule the ends of the earth." When
a beautiful young lady of the blood royal, Julia was
brought in to be cast to the wild beasts, a pagan
priest in his sacerdotal robes walks in by her side,
carrying a burning censer, and begging her to recant
and save her life; observing, "Now Julia just drop
incense on this censer one time in honor of the
Roman gods and you shall live; do you not hear the
lions roaring, coming to devour you?" She responds, "I do, but I also hear the angels singing;
they have come for me and I will quickly fly away
to my loved ones gone on before."

(d) These awful bloody tragedies move on 253
years; meanwhile the Christians run to the end of
the earth to save their lives and go preaching with
all their might everywhere. If I should find that the
people are going to kill me I would run away to save
my life for God as it does not belong to me. But
if they should intercept me so I could not get away
I would go to shouting, the happiest old man you
ever saw; unutterably delighted with the privilege
of dying for Him who has already died for me.
These awful massacres at Rome drove the Christians
in all directions; but they all went preaching the
Word with all their might. Hence you see martyrdom was the very thing to spread the Gospel all
over the world as there were great roads from Rome
leading into every nation under heaven. Nobody
then thought about traveling money, as they had no
public conveyances, but all went on foot.

Thus 253 years of blood and death at the lions'
mouth have passed away. The Emperor Constantine is leading his army on his marches and sees a
golden cross suspended in the firmament, bright as
the sun and superscribed, **en tontoo nilsa,** consequently this. Heeding the divine warning, he halts
his army, takes down the ensigns of the pagan gods
and erects that of the cross. Marching on he soon

arrives in a town and finds the Christians running a tent meeting; falls into it and get gloriously converted. While a lot of his officers and soldiers fall in with him, turning Christians. Others feel awfully disgusted and ashamed of him, and especially the Patricians of the royal blood. When the news flies back. to Rome, that the Emperor has turned Christian, it is a thunder-bolt from a cloudless sky, producing an awful excitement, so the nobility and the royalty rage and actually repudiate the Emperor and go to fighting him, to put him out of office; thus inaugurating a terrible civil war, shaking the empire from center to circumference.

(e)   A number of battles have been fought and the conflict is terrible; the excitement rolling like a mighty ocean wave throughout the empire, which was the whole known world; everything is culminating in a terrible bloody conflict, to decide the fate of mankind. Maximian, the leader of the rebels, vows to Jupiter, the chief Roman god, that if he will give him the victory over Constantine in the on coming battle, he will never stop till he kills every Christian on the globe. The battle comes off; the earth is deluged with blood and heaped with the slain, but Constantine whips him; thus bringing Christianity, so long down-trodden, despised and murdered, to the front of the world. Now Constantine does his best to get everybody to join the Christian Church. His motive is good, but his judgment not unimpeachable. He does his best to stop all idol worship in Rome, but cannot do it to save his life, because during her 753 years conquest of all nations, they had constantly adopted the gods and erected for them temples in Rome. In order to reconcile their devotees. Consequently Rome was crowded with heathen temples, many of them standing to this day as I have seen them.

(f)   Therefore he went a thousand miles toward

the rising sun, lighting down on the Bosporus, connecting the Mediterranean and Euxine Seas and separating Europe and Asia; a most auspicious location for the world's capital. Byzantium had been there a thousand years but never grown much. Now he makes up his mind to found a new capital for the world; walking round and laying off seven mountains, because Rome was built on seven and naming the city New Rome. A vast multitude followed him meanwhile and marked every place where he put his foot down, there to build the wall; wonderfully elated with enthusiasm, knowing that the world's capital would make them rich. Though he did his best to call it New Rome; in their enthusiasm they would name it for him, Constantinople—city of Constantine. He rigidly prevented all heathen temples from erection in the city. In his enthusiasm to get everybody to join the Christian Church, he called a great counsel at Nice, Bythinia and presided over it in person, sitting in a golden chair. He had them formulate a creed for all Christendom, known in history as the Nicene Creed and used this day by the great Catholic Church; the Episcopal creed being a modification of it, and the Methodist's a modification of that. Thus the Nicene is the mother of all the creeds throughout Christendom. Their motives were good; but they made a great mistake as it has proved the glut which has been splitting the log of Christianity ever since. They should have adopted the New Testament as their creed forever. "Why not the Old and New—the whole Bible?" From the simple fact that everything in the Old is substantially and focally revealed in the New which is so small that everybody can learn it. Consequently they only have to thoroughly study the New and then the great volume of the Old as they have opportunity, in order to enjoy the full benefit of God's wonderful revelation, by which we are all saved, sanctified, fed,

panoplied and will all be judged in the great day.
(g)   If they had never made a creed, the Christians would never have differentiated so widely, to the grief of the Holy Spirit, and detriment of the Lord's kingdom. The Nicene Creed is really theology from a pagan standpoint, arising from the fact that under the potent influence of Constantine, millions from all the paganistic organizations, worshipping the host of polytheistical divinities poured into the the Church; their great temples transformed into Christian sanctuaries; their priests turning preachers and the people filling the pews and constituting the membership. The Catholic Church to-day is not only paganistic but full of idolatry. The Calvanistic creed is from the standpoint of election and predestination, which are paganistic as the heathen literature all abounds in unconditional election, and absolute predestination. Homer is not only the first poet in the world but the greatest who has ever been on the earth. He wrote nearly three thousand years ago; whereas the Pentateuch of Moses was only written 3581 years ago. [I have repeatedly had it in my hand, the Book of Job claiming the seniority of the whole world, having preceded the Pentateuch nine years.] In Homer's writing, both Illiad and Odyssey, we have strong affirmations of election and predestination; e. g., Achilles wrath,

To Greeks the direful spring,
Of woes unnumbered, heavenly goddess, sing;
That wrath, which hurled to Pluto's gloomy reign,
The souls of mighty chiefs, untimely slain;
Whose bones unburied on the naked shore
Devouring dogs and hungry vultures tore.

Declare. oh! muse in what ill-fated hour,
Sprang the fierce wrath from what offended power?
Satan's son a dire contagion spread,

And heaped the camp with mountains of the dead.
Since great Atrides and Achilles strove,
Such was the sovereign power, and such the will of
    Jove.

(h)   In this beautiful poetry by Homer you see
positively proclaimed the doctrine of election and
predestination, which has always been prominent
among the heathen.   The Koran of Mohammed
abounds in it; keeping it at the front all the time
and such was the effect on the warriors during the
Moslem conquests for the subjugation of the whole
world to the false prophet; predicted by the seer of
Patmos in the first woe (Rev. 9: 1-12), which lasted
as you see, five months, i. e., 150 years, as a day
stands for a year, and wound up with the battle of
Tours in France, A. D. 733, and the second woe fol-
lowing it to the end of the chapter, which lasted a
year, a month and a day, i. e., 400 years and wound
up with their signal and memorable defeat at Vienna,
Austria, A. D. 1683, when John Sobieschi, with his
seventy thousand Polish warriors signally defeated
and put them to flight.   Meanwhile it is estimated
that they slew 100,000,000 of Christians, throughout
all these bloody centuries; while it seemed that they
certainly would take the whole world and exterminate
Christianity from the globe, the doctrine of absolute
predestination, as taught in the Koran, was the
grand incentive that made them fight with utmost
desperation; solidly believing that they were immortal till their time came to die and also inspired by
the encouraging words of the Koran: "If you fall in
battle your sins are forgiven and in the Judgment
Day your wounds will be resplendent as vermillion,
and odiferous as mush."

The Episcopal creed is Calvanistic and from it we
still have some errors in the English version.   Where
we read in the last chapter of Acts, Paul preaching

to the Jews in his hired house in Rome, quoting
Isaiah the prophet, in E. V., "Seeing, you shall see
and shall not perceive," should read, "may not perceive." "Hearing you shall hear and shall not understand," should read, "may not understand." If they
had been true to the light they might have seen the
Christhood of Jesus and understood it and thus es-
caped the awful doom which overtook them in their
tribulation, i. e., expatriation from their country and
denationalization and worst of all, the loss of their
immortal souls.

Chapter II.

WHERE ART THOU ANCHORED?

We now proceed this momentous question. Take the great paganistic world, 900 million of immortal souls, the apostasy of the Patriarchal Church, all looking to their poor, debauched priests and their dumb idols to save them. Therefore you see where their anchor has gone; it has no hold on the Rock of Ages cleft for me and for you, into which every anchor having been cast, by the lovely angel the glorious hope of a blessed immortality, or rather that hope is the anchor, and cast thither by triumphant, doubtless faith, taking hold of that great Rock, which underlies the broad ocean of this world and actually holds it up, as we see in Matthew 16: 18 when Jesus says, "On this Rock I build My Church and the gates of hell shall not prevail against it, I will give unto thee the keys of the kingdom of heaven and whatsoever thou shalt bind on earth shall be bound in heaven and whatsoever thou shalt loose on earth shall be loosed in heaven. Whosoever sins ye remit are remitted unto him and whosoever sins ye retain are retained unto him." This is the foundation of Catholicism. They claim that Jesus built the Church on Peter and gave him the keys, and he was the first pope. So he transmitted the keys to his successors and they have come down through all ages and the pope yet has the key power to open the kingdom and admit whom he may and remit the sins of whom he may or retain them as he wills. The Catholics stoutly contend that God has thus delegated all the power to the pope, letting it go out of his own hands, and the pope transmits it to his cardinals, and they to the archbishops, and they to the bishops, and they to the millions of priests, who transmit it to whom they will, if you will give them money enough. Hence this is the appalling traffic in the souls of the people.

(i) This is all a horrific perversion of God's truth magnated in the bottomless pit for the damnation of millions. There never was a pope till the seventh century when Procas, the king of Italy, anointed Boniface III., Supreme Pontificate of all the churches and he became the first pope; Peter having been playing on his golden harp among the angels 500 years. In that scripture we have two words which mean rock: **Petros** means a broken rock, blasted out of the quarry and as Peter's name was Simon, when Jesus first met him He gave him the surname, Peter, which is this word **Petros**, and means a broken rock, such as you see all around you in the buildings. He proceeds to state, "On this Rock I will build up My Church and the gates of hell shall not prevail against it." Whereas **Petros** is masculine gender, and applies to Peter; **Petra** is feminine gender and does not mean a broken rock, but the great unbroken stratum which underlies the whole earth; holding up the continents with their great mountain ranges and mighty cities; also underlying all the oceans and seas with their swelling floods. It is feminine· gender because the atonement Christ made is the mother of all God's children and included in this Rock. The Church had been on the earth in all ages. We read of it back in the wilderness and even in the days of Abel, who from it mounted up to heaven from the fratricidal club. John 11: 53 says that Christ will gather into one, the children of God which had been scattered abroad in all ages. Salvation has been in reach of every soul born into the world and living in it on the simple condition that he would walk in the light; as in that case the Blood would cleanse him from all sin (1 John 1: 7.) Therefore in all ages the soul walking in all the light of God's Spirit, providence and his own conscience, has been saved by the Blood, applied by the Holy Spirit, who has always been on the earth, even before man was created, moving on the face of the waters.

(j) When Jesus came on the earth, then the Church, which hitherto had been everywhere dispersed, was established on the great truth of His Christhood, and subsequently no one can be saved who repudiates that truth, as He has always been the only Savior. Therefore when He said, "On this Rock I build My Church," it was His own Christhood, the only foundation of the Church. As Peter was the Senior Apostle and their speaker, representing all the balance, He addresses him personally, "I give unto thee the keys of the kingdom of heaven." If you will read on you will find the plural pronoun used including all the apostles. The keys here are simply His precious Word, which He gave to His Apostles and their successors forever. We all have them now. When we faithfully preach the Word and the people receive it gladly, the normal result is that the door of the kingdom comes open to every appreciative soul, who has nothing to do but enter in; whereas in case of those who reject it, the normal effect is to close the door against them and they are forever locked out. In that way we preachers use the keys of the kingdom to loose the sins from the people, and also to bind them. Oh, how deplorable the infatuation of the poor Catholics anchored in popery, prelacy and priestcraft, looking to the debauched clergy to take away their sins, meanwhile themselves the worst sinners among them. It is simply horrific beyond all conception. Hence you see the appalling attitude of this great multitude of nominal Christians, anchored in the silly sophistries of debauched and wicked sacerdotalism.

(k) Therefore we see 450 millions of people actually anchored in the silly and foolish superstition played off on them by popery, prelacy and priest-craft; meanwhile about nine-tenths of all the Protestant world are Calvanistic, depending on election, predestination and decrees, singing the fond delusion, "Once in grace, always in grace," which our Savior eternally smashes in His parable on the nobleman going away to a far country to receive the kingdom and return (Luke 19: 11), calling up all of his servants and giving each one pound and telling him to make all he can till he comes and he found one who had wrapped his pound in a napkin and kept it nice and clean; never having invested it and giving it a chance to make something for his Lord, thus believing "once in grace always in grace" and practicing what he preached. What was the result? Why, He ordered them to take it from him and give it to the one who had ten; then binding him hand and foot, to cast him into outer darkness, where there is weeping, wailing and gnashing of teeth.

Here you see clearly demonstratively and indisputably refuted, the magnitudinous and favorite dogma, "Once in grace always in grace," as this man lost his grace and his soul too; the former taken from him and given to the ten pounder and the latter cast into hell. Here you see the horrific doom of the millions girdling the globe in every land and nation, anchored in that seductive, captivating and popular doctrine. My mind now lights on Holiness people who long flamed, leaped and shouted the victory and preached with the Holy Ghost sent down from heaven; now like Samson shorn of his locks on the lap of Delila, bereft of their power, unction and victory, lying on the shelf, Ichabod superscribed on their foreheads; having fallen back on that halucinating and captivating downy bed of carnal security, depending on their old experiences, now withered leaves, faded flowers and blighted fruits, to carry them through.

(l)   Methodism was a sunburst on the whole world almost 100 years. But the millions poured in; she took them on board; the ship began to sink, the cry roaring out, "Life boat! Life boat!" God in His infinite mercy, fifty years ago, threw out Free Methodism: really a stalwart iron-clad boat which has stood the storm and rescued millions from the watery, winding sheets and internment in the chasms of the dark, stormy deep. She was thronged and overcrowded, so Wesleyan Methodism came to her relief and the two have been scouring the seas and everywhere gathering up the wreckers, having leaped from the great and overcrowded Methodist ship, in a forlorn effort to escape for their lives before they go down in the dismal whirlpool, which has long ago swallowed the patriarchal, Mosaic and Apostolic churches in the voracious man of Paganism, Mohammedanism, Judaism and great Babylonian Catholicism.

(m)   Thus seeing our lovely Methodism side-tracked, derailed, ditched and stranded on the rough rocks of Satan's fandangoes; the seductive whirlpools of socialism, legalism and lodgery; clandestinely creeping in, like the stealthy vampire, moving over the earth with profound silence; approaching the midnight sleeper, wrapped in the ambrosial mantle of lethean slumber; insinuating his tentacles through the pores of the skin; imbibing the life blood to satisfy his voracious appetite; meanwhile fanning the unsuspecting victim of certain and speedy death; so adroitly soothing the fainting body with the gentle zephyrs, undulating soothingly around him, till the heart, evacuated by the life blood, beats the last time. Such is the wonderful chicanery of Satan, creeping into churches like the midnight vampire in his protean metamorphisms, each cognominal some

imparant philanthropic institution; actually under-
mining the great work of the Holy Ghost; stealing
away His gold, like Shishak, king of Egypt, spoli-
ated the golden shields out of the temple, whose
place Rehoboam supplied with brazen shields.
The shield means faith, the basel grace, by which
we have the victory. Satan clandestinely and adroitly manipulates it away, substituting the brass in its
place. God alone can make gold, which is one of
the original elements He made when He created
the world, while brass, a compound of zink and
Copper, is man's work and as these elements are
cheap, we have no trouble to make all the brass we
want, which shines so brilliantly that uncircum-
cised eyes will never detect it but take it for pure
gold every time. The Church of God has no insti-
tutions but those of the Holy Ghost: His nine graces
by which we are saved (Gal. 5: 19), love, joy, peace,
longsuffering, kindness, goodness, faith, meekness,
and temperance [practical Holiness.] As God is
love (1 John 4: 8,16), therefore all of these other
eight graces are simply metamorphisms of divine
love, as there are two words in the Greek Testament
translated love: **agape,** which means the divine nature. We receive it in regeneration and it is made
perfect in sanctification. The other is **philia,** which
has no salvation in it and is native in the carnal
heart, normal to sinners and even to the animals.
Dives was full of it while in hell, showing up the
fact that we may have it even in its fulness and lose
our souls. Satan deludes people; manipulating this
carnal love on them as a substitute for divine love,
without which there is no salvation.

(n) In this catalogue of the nine graces, joy is
love exultant, leaping and shouting; peace is love
resting sweetly in the arms of Jesus, like the baby,
perfectly safe in its mamma's arms and free from
every care. Long suffering is the burning stake or

lion's mouth, sealing their faith with their blood.
kindness is love like the Good Samaritan, overflowing
and running around hunting somebody whom he can
comfort, brighten and bless.   Goodness is a very
simple, but strong word, as God is simply an abbre-
viation of good.   Hence goodness is the godliness in
us, scattering sunshine, hope, in separation and bless-
ings superabundantly, everywhere we go.   Meekness
is love, sitting on the bottom of the valley of humili-
ation amid blooming flowers, ripening fruits and
copious harvest on all sides, as we always find the
richest and most productive soil in the bottom of the
valley; meanwhile the sweeping tornadoes pass
harmless over our heads.

> The bolt that strikes the popular dead,
> Passes harmless o'er the gentle Hazel's head.

Meanwhile the meek have the glorious ultimus
promise to inherit this world, after Jesus has de-
stroyed sin out of it, driven the devil off and
restored it to the paradiscal state.   (Matt. 5:5.)
"Temperance" rarely love doing God's will on earth
as the angels do it in heaven.   The word is entirely
too weak to reveal the inspired original, **egkratia,**
from **ego,** I, and **kratos,** government.   Therefore the
word means that beautiful self-government which
keeps us perfectly obedient like little Samuel, who
responded to the Lord when He spoke to him: "Speak
Lord, for Thy servant heareth."   Without these
nine graces no one can be saved.   Without the nine
gifts of the Holy Spirit, we may get to heaven
squeezed in by the skin of the teeth (1 Peter 4:18),
but have no reward after we get there, as we have
done nothing for which to be rewarded.   We will
have heaven and all eternity in which to grow in
grace.   Therefore we will be in wonderfully good fix:
but would have been in infinitely more felicious in-

vironments if we had obeyed our Savior: "Lay not
up for yourselves, treasures in earth where moth and
rust doth corrupt; thieves break through and steal:
but lay up treasures in heaven, where neither moth
nor rust corrupt nor theives break through and
steal: for where your treasure is, there will your
heart be also." (Matt. 5: 19.)

(o) We can never do much in the fulfillment of
this commandment unless we have the Lord's pano-
ply, the gifts of the Spirit, wisdom, knowledge, faith,
bodily healing, manipulation of dynastic prophecy,
discernment of spirits, tongues, interpretations of
tongues. These constitute the implements of our
holy warfare, by which we wage an exterminating
war against Satan and his kingdom. Therefore we
cannot afford to dispense with them, but must have
them in order to lay up treasures in heaven. Without them we lose our life-work and at best get to
heaven in spiritual infancy without a reward. The
first gift is wisdom, which means the right use of
our knowledge.

One hundred and fifty years ago, an Irish family
migrated to America, ultimately pitching their tent
in the wild woods of Kentucky. The baby having
lived long enough for them all to fall in love with it,
breathes its life away. As it had never been baptized, they think it is in the fires of purgatory burning.
They ransack all the settlement hunting a priest to
get it out; run on a squatter who tells them there is
no priest in all the land, but a circuit rider comes
around once a month and he is the best they can
do; observing at the same time, "He may be a priest
for ought I know and the very man you want." The
broken-hearted people respond, "Do hunt him up and
send him to us, as the dear baby is burning in purgatory and we want a priest to get it out." Fortunately the cicruit rider James Howe, having been
sent out by Bishop Asbury from the Baltimore Con-

ference, happens to be in that part of his round and meets the squatter, who faithfully delivers his message. Turning his horse toward the Irish cabin, he is soon knocking at the door. They respond. He says, "I am the circuit rider you sent for." They respond, "We want a priest to get the dear baby out of purgatory! Are you a priest?" (Here you see wisdom comes in. If he had said , no, he would have lost the job. Therefore he said ,yes, which was true, as all Holy Ghost preachers are priests forever after the order of Melchizedek.) Therefore he said yes. To make the matter sure they repeat the question: "Are you a Roman Catholic priest?" Now he is in a dilemma; if he says no, he loses the job, if he says yes, he tells a falsehood; so here you see the gift of wisdom again. He answers them, "Not exactly, but I can do anything and everything that a Roman Catholic priest can do." That satisfied them, supposing that priests in this new country were called circuit riders. In their superstitious feeling that every Catholic priest can get people out of purgatory, they gladly turned over to him the job: observing. "Do please get the baby out of purgatory." He then responds, "I am happy to say to you that the baby is not in purgatory (as I have had this matter before God) but in heaven and its the prettiest thing you ever saw. It has never cried a whimper since it got there and angels all want it in their arms at the same time."

(p) They almost die of joy and say, "Holy Father, please come back and see us." Here you see wisdom again: though he preached constantly he had no meeting house, but preached in the cabins of the settlers and under the green trees. Therefore at once concluding the idea of making the Irish cabin one of his appointments he says out right, "Look for me one month from to-day." He publishes the appointment everywhere in his meetings. The day rolls around; the Irish cabin is overflowed with the red hot Methodists gathered far and near, as he was the only Methodist preacher in the state. (I say red hot as there were no other kind of Methodists in the world; the devil having not yet invented the Methodist ice factory.) They throw their mouths open like alligators and roar like lions, the glorious full salvation rings, while fire baptized prayers climb the skies and bring down heavenly avalanches on the people. Sure enough the Lord comes in a Pentecostal cyclone, knocks them all down. They lie prostrate on the floor and cry aloud to God. He sends salvation in showers, bursting heavenly whitecaps. They leap and shout for joy. The whole family gets saved, join the Methodist Church and turn into preachers and from that day have been running to the ends of the earth, preaching the Gospel with the Holy Ghost sent down from heaven.

The writer of this book is one of those preachers, as that was my family on my dear mother's side; my paternity having come from England.

(q) Knowledge is the next gift in the catalogue of nine (1 Cor. 8: 11) and means insight into divine truth, that is the Holy Ghost that made it alone can give. This gift does not preclude our own predicious study, as God commands us , (2 Tim. 2: 15), "Study to show thyself approved of God a workman not to be ashamed."

The next gift is faith. We are all saved by the grace of faith alone as it is the hand by which we receive everything from God; but we save others by the gift of faith, through the wonderful availability of His infallibility, "As your faith is so be it unto you." Hence this gift of faith is invaluable and indispensible.

The next gift is bodily healing, which we all need, not only for our own health, but that we may be a blessing to others all around us. This world is full

of suffering invalids on all sides. When the Lord
sent out the twelve, and again the seventy, He commands them not only to cast out the demons, i. e.,
get people converted, but heal the sick. You will
find the ministry of healing the most available aux-
iliary of soul-saving in all your labors of love. See
my book, "Divine Healing."

Now we come to the gift in E. V. denominated,
"working miracles"; better translated, "the manipulation of dynamites," which is the very word in the
original and the only definition of Gospel in the
Bible. (Rom. 1: 16): "The Gospel is the dynamite
of God unto salvation to every one that believeth."
Dynamite is the greatest mechanical power in all the
world. The only thing in the universe that can
blow the devil out, as in regeneration, and blow out
devil nature, i. e., depravity, as in sanctification.
Oh, how we should be filled with this gift, walking
dynamiters, so as to blow the devil out with all the
people with whom we come in contact; as in case
of the hard, rough man in New York, mentioned by
Bro. John Hatfield, who broke out the windows of a
railroad officer because he prayed so fervently and
shouted so loudly and sang so sweetly, delightfully
receiving all the persecutions of his ungodly neighbor. God came to his relief, put His afflicting hand
on the son who cried for mercy and got saved. The
persecuting father not only was reached but repent-
ed and called in his railroad neighbor to pray for
them all, but moved on and himself got gloriously
saved. This shows up demonstration of the Gospel
dynamite.

Now follows prophecy, which is a regular preacher's gift and we cannot think of doing without it,
as full salvation makes us all preachers, so thrillingly
illustrated in the eighth chapter where we see all
the Pentecostians as they ran from their persecu-
tors, who had killed Stephen, who ran everywhere

preaching the Word. Paul gives the preference, as God has ordained that the world should be saved by preaching. Therefore it is the indispensable **sine qua non.** How shall we preach? "He that prophesieth speaketh unto the people edification, exhortation and comfort." Therefore you see that when ever you are telling a soul the truth of God needed to save him, exhorting him to obey that truth and get saved, or telling him the precious promises of God, thus ministering comfort to his broken heart; then you are preaching the Gospel.

The next gift is "discernment of spirits," which we need in order to know what to preach to every person. If he is a sinner or a backslider, he needs the Sinai Gospel to convict him. If a penitent he needs the Calvary Gospel to convert him. If a justified believer he needs the Pentecost Gospel to sanctify. If he is sanctified he is eligible to translation and needs the transfiguration Gospel to glorify him if he will fly away with the Lord when He comes.

The eighth gift is that of tongues, i.e., languages, which we all need, as language is the vehicle by which Gospel is transmitted to a lost world. Our English Language contains two thousand words. The common people only use three or four hundred, and great scholars only eight or nine hundred; hence you see the vast room of the gifts of the English language. The reason why you don't preach to everybody you meet on the streets, school houses, missions, is because you run out of words. The Holy Ghost will fill you up overflowing so you will never run out, but the more you say the more you will have to say, like a river, deepening and broadening as onward it moves. In this country you need the gift of the English language. If you turn foreign missionary by all means go to the Lord for the language, so you can preach to them without depending on an interpreter; meanwhile study that language with all your might. Remember God sets no premium on laziness but commands us to study. The so-called Tongue Movement is not only full of wild fanaticism, but the counterfeit of evil spirits, giving the noises without any languages; as they have been doing in all the ages, because they cannot give you a language. Isaiah speaks of the wizard as chirping and muttering, so it is nothing new, having been normal to Satan's preacher's in all ages, and now used by the Spiritualists, Mormons and Devil worshippers in heathen lands. It is exceedingly dangerous because these demons are stronger and wiser than we and all aim at our damnation Hence we find the quick and awful apostasy of the Holiness people, who have gone off on the Tongue Movement.

The ninth and last gift is Interpretation. The Lord forbids us to speak in any unknown tongue unless we interpret. I can say with Paul, "I speak with languages more than you all"; but always interpret it so the people can all understand it.

(r) If ye contemplate the whole world, we find the people anchored in their creeds—the mistake of the ages, as we need none but the New Testament, corroborated by the Old which is in perfect harmony with it. The nine hundred millions in their diversified mythological creeds; the three hundred Mohammedans anchored in the false prophet, a fanatical barbarian whom Satan awfully hallucinated under the metamorphism of the archangel, Gabriel, from whom he claims to have seen all his revelations. Besides he was a ferocious, unmerciful, bloody man, in the Koran actually commanding his people, to "kill them," which they did in countless multitudes, everywhere offering them the alternative, the Koran or death. How awful to be anchored in this bloody barbarian, and actually pray to him instead of Jesus. They are exceedingly religious, praying five times

a day. No difference where they are when the time
comes they go at it. How awful to contemplate
four hundred and fifty million anchored in popery,
prelacy and priest-craft depending on the debauched
clergy to take their sins away, themselves the worst
sinners in all the land. The man in the swelling
flood cannot pull any one out of it. Then we have
nine-tenths of the great Protestant world anchored
in the Calvanistical creed and hugging the fond delusion, "once in grace always in grace," Satan's
boa-constrictor choking the life out of them and
blighting the last hope. The Baptists, Presbyter-
ians, Congregationalists, Lutherans and Episcopal-
ians are not only anchored in ecclesiasticisms, but
wound round and round by this great boa-constrictor,
"once in grace always in grace." The mastadonian,
the chain of Satan holding them tight till the cur-
tian drops and doom comes; meanwhile great Methodism, fortunately isolated in the glorious Bible creed
of Christian perfection, since the fatal Zinzendorfian
apostasy, actually left without a creedestical anchor,
till the backslidden preachers manufactured church
lottery, which they are now infelicitously substituting for the Bible battle cry, "Holiness to the Lord."

(r)   Finally let us hear the conclusion of the
whole matter. We must, without hesitation, be anchored in Jesus only in whom dwelleth all the fulness
of the Godhead bodily. (Gal. 2: 8.)   Therefore in
Him we have the Father, Son and Holy Ghost in all
their omniscience and omnipresence and absolutely
everything so we ring out the song: "I've found a
friend in Jesus," etc.

Reader I hope you let your creed and mine and all
others paddle their own canoe and you now and
forever anchor your soul in Jesus and ring out your
song:

My Jesus, I love Thee, I know Thou art mine;
For Thee all the follies of sin I resign;
My gracious Redeemer, my Savior art Thou;
If ever I love Thee, my Jesus 'tis now.

I'll love Thee in life, I will love thee in death,
And praise Thee as long as Thou lendest me breath;
And say, when the death-dew lies cold on my brow,
If ever I love Thee, my Jesus 'tis now.

In mansions of glory and endless delight,
I'll ever adore Thee in heaven so bright;
I'll sing with the glittering crown on my brow,
If ever I love Thee, my Jesus 'tis now.

If not why not utterly and eternally abandon everything to God, and by simple faith take Jesus for everything? Thus anchored in Jesus only, shout the victory.

www.ingramcontent.com/pod-product-compliance
Lightning Source LLC
Chambersburg PA
CBHW030009040426
42337CB00012BA/707